I0504764

Personal Safety Recommendations for
REALTORS

CURTIS KNIGHT

Copyright © 2019 Curtis Knight.

All rights reserved. No part of this book may be reproduced, stored, or transmitted by any means—whether auditory, graphic, mechanical, or electronic—without written permission of the author, except in the case of brief excerpts used in critical articles and reviews. Unauthorized reproduction of any part of this work is illegal and is punishable by law.

The recommendations expressed in this book are the author's views and are based on personal experiences. Use your own discretion before utilizing these recommendations. The information provided in this book is intended to provide helpful personal safety recommendations. The recommendations have validity and have been applied successfully to many personal safety plans. However, all recommendations are made without a guarantee that you won't become a victim of a crime. The author disclaims any liability in connection with the use of these recommendations.

ISBN: 978-1-6847-1155-0 (sc)
ISBN: 978-1-6847-1154-3 (e)

Library of Congress Control Number: 2019916042

Because of the dynamic nature of the Internet, any web addresses or links contained in this book may have changed since publication and may no longer be valid. The views expressed in this work are solely those of the author and do not necessarily reflect the views of the publisher, and the publisher hereby disclaims any responsibility for them.

Any people depicted in stock imagery provided by Getty Images are models, and such images are being used for illustrative purposes only. Certain stock imagery © Getty Images.

Lulu Publishing Services rev. date: 10/17/2019

To Tiffany, my wife, companion, and greatest encourager. Thank you for giving me the time and space needed to create this book. You are the anchor of our family. I'm truly blessed to have you as my wife.

Contents

Introduction

As realtors, implementing crime prevention techniques and strategies into our everyday activities can lead to a reduction in crime. The goal is to make criminal acts harder to commit and get away with by changing how we approach our everyday activities.

Realtors need to take proactive measures to make themselves less likely of becoming a victim of a crime. You stand a much better chance of preventing criminal attacks if you develop a safety plan before you need it. A plan is designed to minimize your risk as well as being prepared for certain situations. Before you interact with a client or enter a home showing, it's important to establish a personal safety plan. Your personal safety plan is a customized strategy for how you will conduct showings, host open houses, interact with clients, and communicate with your office.

Realtors' daily routines take them in a variety of environments and put them in contact with different people, so it's important to always think safety. It's important for realtors to take time to think about their daily routines and identify times and places they could be at risk.

Realtors should never get complacent or have a mind-set that "it can't happen to them." A lot of times, realtors are tempted to make a quick sale, but they have to be conscious of their safety.

The goal of this book is to educate realtors about the risks they face on the job so there is a reduction of harm or injury. The book will also assist realtors with establishing a personal safety plan. Realtors should always be conscious of how they conduct showings and open houses, as well as how they deal with the general public.

Three Components Necessary for a Crime

There are three components necessary for any crime to occur; urge (desire), skill, and opportunity. The equation is:

$$\text{Urge} + \text{Skill} + \text{Opportunity} = \text{Crime}$$

Of these three components, the only one that we can control is opportunity. We can't control a criminal's urge to commit a crime. There's an example I will never forget. Early in my law enforcement care, I remember receiving a call to respond to a belated break-in to a business. Upon arrival at this business, the store owner met me at the front of the store. I could tell that he was very upset. The store was all brick, and it had only one entrance, the front door, which was glass.

However, the glass was not shattered, so I asked the owner of the business, "How did the suspect get in?" He walked me to the backside of the store. Once we were behind the store, he pointed to a large hole in the brick that the suspects had created. It appeared that the suspects had used some type of blunt object to beat a whole in the wall to enter the store.

The store owner told me that once the suspects were inside of the store, they only took maybe thirty to forty dollars' worth of merchandise. The point that I wanted to bring out is that we can't control another person's urge to commit a crime.

We also can't control a criminal's skill level. In society, we have white-collar and blue-collar criminals. White collar criminals are viewed as respectable people who hold high-ranking positions within large companies. They commit mostly nonviolent crimes that cost society millions of dollars each year. Some examples of white-collar crimes are fraud, embezzlement, cybercrimes, and identity theft.

Blue-collar criminals differ from white-collar criminals in that they are from a lower social class of people. Some examples of blue-collar crimes are burglary, shoplifting, sexual assault, and car break-ins. This is something we can't control.

However, we can eliminate the opportunity for a crime to occur. Many real estate agent attacks are crimes of opportunity. A few examples of eliminating opportunity for an attack to occur include conducting showings during daylight hours, not wearing expensive jewelry during open houses, and never conducting a showing before verifying background information on a client. The goal is to manipulate the opportunity structure to reduce the likelihood that offenders will choose to commit a crime.

Personal Safety Risks
That Realtors Face

Real estate agents face many personal safety risks simply by the nature of the profession. They are exposed to violent and property crimes. Realtors are at higher risk of on-the-job crime than most professions. This is because realtors work with the general public, travel to neighborhoods they are not familiar with, project an image of success, multitask while driving, and work alone with complete strangers for long periods of time in vacant homes. The risk of harm or injury may increase when working alone because of the difficulty in contacting the police or someone for help; they often can't be seen or heard. When realtors spend time with strangers, the risk of personal and property victimization increases.

Real estate is a competitive business. When you get a phone call from a potential client, you subconsciously want to rush out and start the transaction. Many agents immediately start thinking about their commission check and begin planning for their next trip to Hawaii! However, it's very important to think about your personal safety first. Don't meet clients at a property before properly screening them.

There is also a myth that only woman agents are at risk of becoming victims of a crime. That's incorrect. Men agents are at risk as well. A predator doesn't care whether you are a male or female agent. Your experience as a realtor doesn't make you more or less likely to become a victim of a crime.

Some of the crime risk that realtors are exposed to on a daily basis include assault, carjacking, harassment, homicide, kidnapping, larceny, motor vehicle break-ins, murder, rape, robbery, road rage, stalking, threats, and theft.

Property Crimes

Larceny

Motor vehicle break-in

Theft

Vehicle theft

Violent Crimes

Assault

Carjacking

Homicide

Hostage

Kidnapping

Murder

Rape

Robbery

Open House Safety Recommendations

Conducting an open house in a safe manner is very important. There are several inherent safety risks that realtors are exposed to when hosting an open house. Realtors sit in empty houses, waiting on strangers to arrive. These strangers could possibly be predators. There is no screening process, so realtors don't know when a predator or a legitimate buyer has entered the house. Realtors advertise days (and even weeks) in advance when and where they will be hosting an open house. This gives the criminal plenty of time to plan an attack.

When realtors market their open houses, they should also advertise that security will be on hand, video surveillance will be in use, or ID will be required. Also say that registration is required to attend your open house. Allow prospects to RSVP through your office or telephone.

That way, you can at least screen who will attend your open house.

When hosting an open house, realtors can implement the following safety practices to make themselves and the homeowner less likely of becoming a victim of a crime: arrive early, invite a fellow agent to attend, communicate with the office, alert sellers about their valuables, and close properly.

Arrival

When hosting an open house, it's very important to arrive a few hours prior to the start time. By arriving early, realtors can become familiar with the neighborhood, invite the neighbors, and inspect the property. The neighbors are trusted people who are invested in the community.

Upon arrival, it's important to conduct a sweep of the exterior and interior of the subject property. An exterior sweep of the property includes scanning behind ambush locations like overgrown bushes and shrubs. Always check windows to make sure they are secure. When checking a window, if one is open or broken, don't go inside because an unauthorized person could have broken into the property. Also, if it is a break-in, you don't want to contaminate the crime scene. The exterior sweep also includes checking inside sheds, crawl spaces, storage units, and any other exterior locations where someone could hide.

Once you have inspected the exterior of the home and everything checks out, you can then start your interior sweep of the property. Upon approaching the front door, check to make sure it is secure. If the door is open, don't go inside because it could possibly be a break-in. When you first enter the property, announce who you are so that if for some reason the homeowners are home, they will know that it's not someone trying to break into their home. Once you are inside of the home, check all areas where someone could hide. Check places like closets, washer and dryer areas, under beds, behind chairs, and under tables. It's also a good practice to open all blinds and turn on all lights.

Once the interior sweep is complete, the next most important thing to do is note all the entrances and exits to the property. The goal is to establish your escape routes from each level of the house. These locations could be the front entrance, the back entrance, side doors, windows, or garage doors. If a window is one of your escape routes, know in advance how high it is from the ground in case you need to jump. Wherever you decide, make sure that you know ahead of time where you are going once you exit the house. It's always a good practice to establish a minimum of three escape routes.

Invite Fellow Agents

When planning and organizing an open house, invite other agents to attend. Invite a new agent from your office; he or she is usually looking for these opportunities. It's wise to work in pairs during an open house. That way, you won't be in an empty house for several hours by yourself, waiting to meet complete strangers. Multiple agents provide more eyes to be on alert for criminal activity. If no agent in your office is available to assist, you can always invite a lender, builder, spouse, or appraiser to accompany you.

Communicate with Your Office

When hosting an open house, it's very important to let someone from your office know where you are at all times. Give your office or a fellow agent your location, time, and date for your open house. It's good to have people on standby whom you can call every so often to let them know that you are okay. If possible, coordinate with the sellers (if they are still living in the home) to see if they could arrive twenty minutes before the scheduled end time of your open house. Never host an open house without letting someone know where you are.

Alert Sellers about Their Valuables

During an open house, there is no way to determine who is coming through the door. There is not enough time to do a background check on everyone who walks in. Everyone should enter through a monitored entrance and should be acknowledged and greeted. Any open house can attract many visitors. Realtors can limit the amount of guests in at one time. Even then, a realtor may not be able to watch everyone at all times.

Open houses give criminals an opportunity to tour someone's house and steal property. They also allow criminals to case the house to see what valuables are inside so that they can come back at a later time and break in. This is why it's very important to remind your sellers to remove valuables that can be easily stolen. Examples of valuables that should be removed are expensive paintings, computers, expensive jewelry, financial documents, expensive cloths, family photos, electronics, and prescription medication. Remind your sellers to update their home insurance policies. Also, advise your sellers to create an inventory sheet.

An inventory sheet (see the appendix) is one of the most important crime-prevention documents that you can recommend to your sellers. The sheet is important to have because if something is stolen and found, it can be traced back to the person. Most people don't walk around with serial numbers stored in their heads. For example, if someone attends an open house and steals a computer, the first thing the seller is going to do is file a police report. When the police officer comes to file the report, one of the first things the officer will ask for is the serial number. If you have the serial number, the officer can enter the number into the National Crime Information Center (NCIC) database. This is an FBI database. Once the serial number is entered into NCIC, it lists the property as stolen nationwide. Nine times out of ten, the criminal will try to take the stolen property to a pawn shop. If the criminal tries to pawn the stolen item and it has been entered into NCIC, it will register as stolen. The pawn shops can then notify the police, and the victim can get back the property.

Advise your sellers to record all of their valuables that have a serial number (laptops, televisions, iPads, etc.) onto the inventory sheet. The inventory sheet should have a space for the make of the item, brand, color, and serial number. Recommend to the sellers that they invest in an engraver for the items that don't have a serial number. Tell them to engrave their initials or any characters that will help identify their property if stolen.

Once all of the serial numbers or identifiable characters have been recorded on the inventory sheet, they should store it in a safe and easily accessible place. My recommendation is to advise the sellers to take a photo of the sheet and e-mail it to themselves. You can also give a copy of the sheet to a trusted loved one.

Closing the Open House

When closing the open house, one of the most important things to remember is to conduct another sweep of the house to check whether anyone is left inside of the house. The sweep should be done with at least two agents, if possible. Check all windows and doors to make sure they are secure. Criminals may unlock windows and doors so that they can return later.

It's important to stick to your scheduled closing time. If someone arrives at your open house minutes before you close, advise that person to schedule a private showing with you.

Additional Open House Recommendations

- Live stream your open house.
- Don't leave belongings unattended.
- Keep your phone fully charged.
- Invite the neighbors to the open house.
- Store sharp objects like knives and fireplace pokers.
- Don't have your head buried in your phone or electronic devices.
- Never advertise a property as being vacant.
- Post a sign at the entrance that the property is under surveillance.

Showing Safety Recommendations

When realtors are scheduled to show a property, there are many opportunities for a criminal to commit a crime against them. Meeting strangers at a vacant house can expose an agent to many dangerous situations. It's important to have a safety routine when showing a property.

Meet at the Office First

Before you show a property to any potential client, it's very important to first meet the client at your office. When meeting the client at the office, verify that the person has a prequalification letter from a lending institution. Never show a property to anyone without the prequalification letter; it will save you time and it will also keep you safe.

There is no need to show a property if the client is not qualified to buy a house. You can also ask for references in regard to employment; call them to verify how the person is.

While at the office with the client, make a copy of the person's driver's license, vehicle registration, and prequalification letter. Before you start working with potential clients, get as much information as possible about them. If the clients are going to invest that much money to buy a house, they shouldn't be reluctant to provide you with this information. Don't be in a hurry to show a property without verifying who someone is. Never meet anyone whom you have not verified at a house for a showing.

When you can't meet at your office, ask a lender, home inspector, title company, or attorney if you can use the person's office. These people are all real estate partners.

Showing the Property

Just like an open house, when you have scheduled a showing, it's best to arrive before the actual showing time. However, you may not be able to arrive hours in advance to inspect the property like an open house. This is because with a showing, there may be other agents who have scheduled showings for the same property before you. You can still arrive ahead of your scheduled time. It's very important to get to know the property, including the entrances, and exits to the community.

Upon arrival, always park on the street near the house. Never park near dead-end streets or in driveways. This will eliminate you being trapped if you need to leave quickly in an emergency situation. Just like when you arrive at an open house, you should conduct an exterior and interior sweep of the property. The exterior sweep should include identifying ambush locations like overgrown bushes and shrubs, sheds, storage units, and anywhere someone could hide. Check all windows as well to make sure they are secure.

Before you conduct the interior sweep of the property, knock or ring the doorbell of the house before entering the house. Announce who you are in case the homeowner is still there. Many agents have encountered squatters when they have entered a home for a showing. Squatters are those who are living on the property but do not have permission to be there. They have committed at least two crimes: breaking and entering, and trespassing. If you encounter squatters or find something that seems suspicious upon entering the property, back out and call the police.

Reporting Suspicious Activity

When calling the police to report a squatter or any suspicious activity, there are five Ws that you should remember.

1. Who
2. What
3. Where
4. When
5. Weapons

When you call the police, the communicator is going to ask you for these five Ws. Most people forget to mention weapons. It's very important to advise the communicator whether or not a weapon is involved in a crime. This is because when the police get on scene, they need to know what they are getting themselves into. For example, let's say you encounter a squatter who has a firearm and attempts to rob you.

When you call the police, you need to let the police know because they may be a block away. Let's say that you gave the communicator this information, the police see the suspect running from the house, and it's 3:00 p.m. on a Wednesday afternoon. The police give chase to the squatter and eventually apprehend the squatter, but the squatter doesn't have that firearm. What does that mean? It means that he or she probably threw the firearm somewhere. What else does that mean? What normally happens at 3:00 p.m. on Wednesday afternoons? Kids are released from school. This is important to law enforcement because now they have to conduct an article search in order to find that firearm before a small child picks it up.

When calling the police to report a squatter or suspicious activity, remember the approximate age, height, weight, hair color, eye color, clothing, and race. Also, try to look for things that can't change, like scars, marks, tattoos, and voice.

Always report suspicious activity. This builds intelligence for law enforcement and for the next agent who may be showing properties in that neighborhood in the future. If you don't want to get involved, call anyway and remain anonymous.

Additional Showing Recommendations

- Show properties only during daylight hours.
- Never drive clients around in your car.
- Always make sure your phone is charged.
- Avoid basements, attics, and crawl spaces.

- Leave your purse or wallet at home.
- Take a picture of your client/vehicle with your phone.
- Ask owners to secure pets.
- Don't allow in other agents during your showing time.
- Keep up with the house key; properly secure it.
- Secure all doors at the conclusion of the showing.
- Introduce your client to your office manager.
- Call someone every forty-five minutes to let others know you are okay.
- Try not to show properties alone.
- Be aware of the neighborhood and your surroundings.
- Avoid wearing expensive jewelry.
- Meet at an office first. Don't simply pop up at a house.
- Don't go into rooms with one exit.
- Get clients' car information: plate number, make, model.

Vehicle Safety Recommendations

Every minute, a motor vehicle is stolen somewhere in the United States. Motor vehicle theft is one of the top property crimes in the country. Realtors spend a lot of time in their vehicles on their phones and electronic devices. Today, realtors are more wireless and paperless. Carjackings are also on the rise because a lot of cars have the key fob or electronic start mechanism. Carjacking is when someone steals your car while you are in it. In the section, I will discuss several vehicle safety recommendations.

Don't Leave Items Visible

Realtors use many devices to assist them with meeting clients' needs. Many times items such iPads, laptops, cellular devices, client files, and GPS devices are left exposed inside cars. Some criminals case neighborhoods looking for items like these to steal. Never leave items exposed in your vehicle. Always roll your windows completely up and lock your doors.

Never Leave a Vehicle Running

It's very important to never leave your vehicle running if you are not in it, even if you have a remote starter installed in your car. Leaving your vehicle running unattended gives thieves an opportunity to steal it. A stolen car presents considerable hazards to road safety. A stolen car is more likely to be involved in a car crash than one that is not stolen. If your vehicle is ever stolen, report it immediately. Have a good description of your vehicle as well (VIN, plate number, make, model, and color).

Vehicle Registration Cards

Most realtors leave their registration cards in their glove box. My recommendation is to put the registration card somewhere else in your vehicle. There is a new high-tech device that criminals are using to break into cars: an electromagnetic pulse (EMP) device. This device is about the size of a cell phone. Criminals are holding this device to the passenger's side door handle, and it unlocks the doors without setting off the alarm. The criminals are targeting registration cards to steal identity information. Millions of Americans every year are affected by identity theft. Also, check your registration plate often to see whether it has been removed. Some criminals steal registration plates and put them on stolen vehicles.

Parking Safely

Parking safely is very important for realtors. When you arrive at your open house or showing, never park in the driveway. This way, you will not be blocked in. Be mindful of dead-end streets. It's wise to park your vehicle facing the exit/entrance points of the streets. It's good practice to park your car so that your driver's side door is facing the front door of the home you are at. That way if you need to run out, you can easily gain entry into your vehicle.

Emergency Safety Kits

As mentioned earlier, realtors spend a lot of time in their vehicles. You never know when you will get a flat tire or when you vehicle may stop working. It's very important to have an emergency kit in your car at all times. Some things that you should keep in your emergency kit are warm clothes, a flashlight, a spare tire, water, food, rain gear, a car jack, a first aid kit, and jumper cables.

Leaving the Property

When you leave your open house or showing, never stand next to your vehicle searching through your pockets or purse for your car keys. Get your keys out and have them in your hand before you leave the property. This is important because if you need to make a quick escape, you won't be delayed.

Additional Vehicle Safety Recommendations

- Don't crack windows, even in the summertime.
- Get your vehicle regularly inspected.
- Know where you are at all times.
- Put your phone down while driving.
- Pack an emergency safety kit.
- Always have your keys in hand when approaching your vehicle.
- Don't sit inside your vehicle to do paperwork.
- Be aware of dead-end streets.
- Always keep your gas tank full.
- Always wear your seatbelt while driving.
- Avoid road rage.

- Never pick up a hitchhiker.
- Be mindful of personalized license plates.
- Check the backseat for criminals when you get in your car.
- If your vehicle is stolen, report it immediately.
- Park on the curb, not in the driveway, at showings and open houses.
- Check your registration plate often. Make sure it hasn't been stolen.

Working from Home Safety Recommendations

Today, many realtors work from home rather than within the confines of an office. When working from home, there are many crime-prevention strategies that realtors should implement into their personal safety plans.

Criminals are not going to spend a lot of time trying break into your home. If they do break in, they are going to spend about three to six minutes inside the house. Where do most women keep their precious diamonds and jewelry? In the jewelry box on the dresser, in the bedroom. When the criminals break into a home, they are more likely to head straight to the bedroom because that's where they are likely to score big. The recommendation here is to put our valuables and important documents in odd places.

Exterior Home Recommendations

If you have small bushes and trees along the perimeter of your property, the recommendation is to implement the "three foot, six foot" rule. The rule centers around cutting your bushes down to about three feet high; this will eliminate any ambush locations for criminals to hide behind. If you have trees along the perimeter of your property, the recommendation is to cut the tree canopy up to about six feet. Cutting the tree canopy will eliminate concealment for criminals.

Exterior Doors

All of your exterior doors should be locked at all times. A solid hardwood door is recommended because if a criminal tries to kick in the door, the door won't give in like a hollow door. Also, check the strike plate on the door frame to ensure you have 2.5- to 3.0-inch screws going into the strike plate. This will make your door more resistant if a criminal tries to kick it in.

Peephole

A lot of new construction homes don't have a peephole. If you live in a home that doesn't have a peephole, get one installed. A peephole will allow you to look out and see who is at your door before you open it. Make sure that the peephole is installed at or below eye level.

Low-Sitting Windows

If you have low-sitting windows along the perimeter of your house, there are several safety tips that you can implement. Plant a row of holly bushes near the window. Criminals may think twice about breaking into that window because they don't want to get pricked by the bush. You can also place a slab of gravel in front of the window. This gravel will make noise when someone tries to enter through the window. Most criminals don't like to be seen or heard when they are committing a crime.

You should remove all expensive items and clutter from the windows. It's is wise to keep your windows clear from clutter. You always want to be able to see from the inside of your home to the outside.

Outside Sheds

Many people today use outside sheds as home offices. Criminals know this. They know that computers, printer, important documents, and other office materials are stored in sheds. I wouldn't recommend using your shed as office space if at all possible.

Porch Pirates

When ordering packages online and having them delivered to your house, be mindful of porch pirates. Porch pirates are criminals who follow behind delivery trucks. Once packages are dropped off, they walk up and steal the packages. Here are some recommendations to prevent porch pirates from stealing your packages.

- Schedule and track your packages.
- Add delivery instructions to not have packages dropped off on the porch.
- Ask a trusted neighbor who will be home to pick it up upon arrival.
- Have the packages delivered to a PO box.
- Have the package delivered to your job.

House Keys

Never engrave your address on your house keys. I had neighbors who had their car stolen. Their house key was on the same key ring as their car key. By the time the police arrived to take their report, the suspects who had stolen their car had already made it to their house and stolen a lot of important documents and electronics.

General Statute for Self–Defense

A lot of people ask me, "What do I do if someone breaks into my home while I'm there?" I always refer them to their state's general statue that governs the use of force in self-defense. In North Carolina, the general statute that governs the use of force in self defense is NC G.S. 14–51.3. The provisions for this statute are easy to find; simply go to Google and type in the statute. The provisions in the statute will clearly define what's allowed and what's not allowed as it pertains to the use of force in a self-defense situation. It's very important to have a plan in place for your family if someone breaks into your house while you are there.

Additional Home Safety Recommendations

- Test your fire alarm often.
- Post pictures from vacation after you return home.
- Keep all windows locked.
- Install security cameras.
- Install flood lights.
- Install alarm systems.

- Make sure your house numbers are visible from the street (for first responders).
- Install new locks when you move into a new home.
- Make sure all entry points are well lit.

Conclusion

This book has covered valuable information as it pertains to realtor safety. Personal safety risk that realtors face daily was discussed. In addition, safety recommendations were made for how to conduct an open house, showing properties to clients, safety when operating a vehicle and safety practices for when realtors work from home.

The real estate profession exposes agents to many safety risks that other professions don't. Realtors meet strangers at vacant homes, travel to environments that they are not familiar with and sit in empty house waiting on complete strangers to walk in. So, it's very important that realtors establish a safety plan for their business. There is **NO** transaction worth risking your life for.

The recommendations that are shared in this book are intended to help keep realtors safe while they perform their daily duties. Never let complacency set in or have the mindset that it can't happen to me.

Appendix

Inventory Spreadsheet

Name					
Telephone Number					
Email Address					
Home Address					
Make	Brand	Color	Model No.	Serial No.	
1.					
2.					
3.					
4.					
5.					
6.					
7.					
8.					
9.					
10.					

www.ingramcontent.com/pod-product-compliance
Lightning Source LLC
Chambersburg PA
CBHW031502210526
45463CB00003B/1042

* 9 7 8 1 6 8 4 7 1 1 5 5 0 *